DERRIDA IN 90 MINUTES

Derrida
IN 90 MINUTES

Paul Strathern

194
str

IVAN R. DEE
CHICAGO

Library of Congress Cataloging-in-Publication Data:
Strathern, Paul, 1940–
    Derrida in 90 minutes / Paul Strathern
       p. cm. — (Philosophers in 90 minutes)
    Includes bibliographical references and index.
    ISBN 1-56663-328-1 (cloth : alk. paper) — ISBN 1-56663-
329-X (pbk. : alk. paper)
    1. Derrida, Jacques.   I. Title: Derrida in ninety minutes.
II. Title.

B2430.D484 S77 2000
194—dc21   00-056963

Contents

Introduction   5

Derrida's Life and Works   9

Derrida: Mixed Quotes and Mixed Reviews   79

Chronology of Significant Philosophical Dates   82

Chronology of Derrida's Life and Times   86

Recommended Reading   90

Index   92

Introduction

"I love nothing better than remembering and Memory itself," claimed Jacques Derrida in his 1984 memoir of his close friend, the philosopher Paul de Man, who had recently died. Yet at the same time Derrida confessed: "I have never known how to tell a story." These two characteristics are far from being contradictory for the author. As he says of himself: "It is precisely because he keeps the memory that he loses the narrative." The image remains "legible"; incorporating it in a "story" inevitably blurs this legibility, imposing interpretation. So far so good. It thus comes as something of a surprise when we discover that the ensuing memoir contains not a single image of his friend and absolutely no memories of him. Needless to say, there is not even a hint of story about him: this would impose interpretation. Yet paradoxically this entire so-called memoir is devoted to an interpretation of his friend's intellectual achievement. In his own words, Derrida "dialogues obliquely" with de Man's work, obscurely interpreting it with regard to "prudent explication" and "a battery of performative acts" by such figures as Heidegger, Austin, Hölderlin, and Nietzsche.

Any clear, commonsense approach to Derrida's work thus labors under a severe disadvantage. Worse still, it goes completely against the author's intention. It is therefore only fair to warn the reader that my attempt at clarity in the ensuing description of Derrida's life and work would be regarded by its author as both counterproductive and hopelessly biased. Wit, on the other hand, is definitely permitted. Derrida is a great believer in jokes, puns, and humor. Yet here again we suffer a setback: this is specifically French intellectual humor. It derives from that modernist tradition of European Continental art and thought known as "the absurd." When confronted with an absurd situation, innocent outsiders living beyond this privileged intellectual territory are wont to laugh. Such naiveté displays a woeful misunderstanding. The absurd is a notion of utmost seriousness. Similarly with Derrida's humor. This is no laughing matter. It is not funny (except to French intellectuals). Such humor doesn't play for laughs. Derrida may share a Jewish background with Woody Allen, but by no stretch of the imagination do they share a common humor. Whether the Manhattan hypochondriac or the great Parisian intellectual sheds more light on our varied humanity—in other words, is more "serious"—is another question.

Derrida's Life and Works

Central to Derrida's "deconstructionist" philosophy is his insistence: "There is nothing outside the text." Despite this, and no matter which textual form it takes, the *fact* that Jacques Derrida was born in Algeria in 1930 would appear to remain impregnable to deconstructive assault. His family were *petit bourgeois* "assimilated" Jews, both part of the French colonial class and yet partial outsiders within it. He grew up in the capital, the seaside city of Algiers. Here the Europeans lived the easygoing empty Mediterranean life revolving between business, café, and beach—so tellingly evoked by the French-Algerian writer and philosopher Albert Camus in *The Outsider.* Derrida lived on rue Saint-

Augustin, a fact that would play a leading yet somewhat serendipitous role in his 1991 autobiography. This he called *Circumfession*, its title implying the two main topics: circumcision and confession. Yet by the end of the work we are left little the wiser about details of either. At one point, apparently referring to himself, Derrida writes: "he circumcises himself, the 'lyre' in one hand, the knife in the other." Yet some pages later he writes: "Circumcision remains the threat of what is making me write here." The confessional element is equally muddied. At one point he addresses the reader with regard to his mother: "I lied to her all the time, as I do to all of you." There follows a long Latin quotation from *The Confessions* of St. Augustine. Derrida's "circumfession" has many Latin quotes from St. Augustine, with whom he seeks to identify. St. Augustine was in fact born in 354 A.D. in the Roman colony of Numidia, whose territory now forms part of Algeria. Other resemblances to the early Christian philosopher and religious confessionist are more fleeting. Besides identifying with St. Augustine, Derrida also fantasizes about him, envisioning the Christian saint "as a little homosexual Jew (from Algiers or New York)," and even refers to his own "impossible homosexuality." At another point he professes: "I do not know Saint Augustine." Having established this much, we can now move on to more factual ground.

In 1940, when Derrida was just ten years old, Algeria was dragged into World War II. Although the country never saw fighting, or even so much as a German uniform, the war cast its pestilential shadow over life in the French colony, which had now become a protectorate of the Nazi empire. Again, Camus captures the atmosphere of the period, this time in *The Plague*. France had been overrun, and French Algeria was governed by the collaborationist Pétain regime. In line with Nazi decrees, in 1942 racial laws were introduced, bringing to the surface a latent anti-Semitism amongst the European population. Derrida was informed by a master at school: "French culture is not made for little Jews." It was the privilege of the top pupil to raise the French flag each morning at school; but in Derrida's case this was reassigned to the second in the class. A quota system was introduced limiting each *lycée* (high school) to 14 percent Jews. Derrida's headmaster soon took it upon himself to reduce this quota to 7 percent, and Derrida was expelled. At street level such attitudes degenerated to name-calling and even violence.

The effect of all this on an exceptionally intelligent, sensitive pupil can only be imagined. It is also equally understandable that the man who emerged from this experience should deny the effect of his early life on his later thought. After all, his avowed aim was to interrogate philosophy, not himself. Consequently he remained averse to supplying personal details that appeared to provide a causal link between his life and his work. And with some justice. It should be remembered that the mature survivor thought out his philosophy *despite* such attempts to sabotage his intellectual and social life.

For a while, the early teenage Jacques received no education. He was enrolled at the unofficial Jewish *lycée* but secretly played truant most of the time. He was aware of "belonging" to Judaism; yet though he had grown up assimilated into European society, he now felt he was not a part of it. His painful experience led him to reject racism of any sort; yet in the words of his collaborator Geoffrey Bennington, he also experienced "impatience with gregarious identification, with the militancy of belonging in general, even if it is Jewish."

Upon the resumption of normal education after the war, Derrida became a disruptive pupil, successful only on the playing field. He dreamed of becoming a professional soccer player. Such an ambition may not have been quite so philistine as it appears. Just over ten years earlier, Camus had played in goal for Racing Algiers. And it was during this period that Derrida overheard, by chance, a talk about Camus on the radio, which attracted him to philosophy. Derrida's hero was a thinking man of action.

Despite his teenage rebellion, Derrida's exceptional intellect remained unmistakable. At nineteen he was sent to Paris to study for entry to the École Normale Supérieure, the most prestigious higher-education establishment in France. But living alone amidst the grey cold streets of Paris proved an alienating experience after the sea and sunlight of Algiers. Derrida found himself drawn to the nihilistic existentialist philosophy of Sartre, which was then all the rage in the student cafés of the Left Bank. Sartre asserted "existence before essence." He maintained that there was no such thing as an essential humanity. Our subjectivity was not given to us: we create it ourselves by our actions. The way we choose to live makes us who we are.

As a result of exam pressure, disorientation, and pill-taking (amphetamines and sleeping pills), Derrida walked out after taking his first exam and suffered a minor nervous breakdown. In 1952, at his second attempt, he gained admission to the École Normale Supérieure, where he studied philosophy for the next five years. Here Derrida began a close reading of the two figures who had most influenced Sartre, the German philosophers Husserl and Heidegger. These early-twentieth-century thinkers had been instrumental in developing and elaborating phenomenology, "the philosophy of consciousness." This insisted that our fundamental consciousness lies beyond the reach of rational proof or scientific evidence. It is accessible only to intuition. By means of this alone we arrive at the central problems of being, of existence itself. The basis of all our knowledge thus lies beyond reason and science: our knowing is grounded in consciousness.

In 1954 the Algerian War broke out when the local Arab and Berber populations rose against the French in a bid for independence. Derrida supported the struggle for independence, but after graduating in 1957 he was called up to serve in Algeria with the French army. He volunteered to teach and was posted outside Algiers to a school for the children of French and Algerian soldiers in the French army. Derrida found himself torn by the increasing atrocities on both sides, but still hoped for an independent Algeria where Europeans could coexist with their Arab and Berber neighbors. Derrida's family had lived in Algeria for more than five generations and regarded themselves as Algerians rather than French. In 1960 he returned to France, where he obtained a post teaching philosophy and logic at the Sorbonne, part of the University of Paris. He was now married to Marguerite Aucoutourier, who had been a fellow student at the École Normale Supérieure. She had accompanied him to Algeria but was unable to prevent him from suffering a severe depressive episode after his return. The war would end with Algeria's independence in 1962 and the mass exodus of Europeans. Derrida's cherished hope of becoming a citizen of an independent Algeria was shattered; from this time on he would frequently experience feelings of what he called "nostalgeria." But 1962 would also see the inception of Derrida's own independence as a philosopher, with the publication of his first important work. To a translation he had made of Edmund Husserl's *Origin of Geometry* he appended a book-length Introduction which dwarfed Husserl's essay-length work.

Husserl had originally been a mathematician, which led him to see the danger of phenomenology basing all knowledge on intuition or the immediacy of individual apprehension. If the basis of all knowledge lay beyond reason and science, how could one know the truth of anything that was not based upon his own intuition? This meant that mathematical and scientific knowledge was relative. Such propositions as $2 + 2 = 4$ were not incontrovertible, they just arose from one's intuition of the world. Others might intuit things differently. In which case one would have no grounds to refute them.

Husserl sought to rescue philosophy from this difficulty, which threatened to undermine all knowledge. He took geometry as the most certain form of our knowledge, using it as a paradigm for all scientific and mathematical knowledge. If our knowledge of geometry could be shown to be beyond relativism, this would secure the truth of all such science.

Husserl argued that geometry must have had a historical origin. Its origin lay in an original intuition by a historical human being. On a particular day in prehistory a particular individual must have had an intuition of line, or distance, or possibly even of a point. In this subjective way geometry—line, distance, point, and so forth—had begun. Such original terms must have had a clear, irrefutable meaning, first grasped by intuition. But once these terms had been grasped by intuition, the rest of geometry was simply a matter of discovering the logical implications of these grounding assumptions. In ancient Greek times Euclid had shown how the structure of geometry was built up from such basic concepts. Geometry itself was somehow "already there," waiting to be discovered, abiding its historical moment. Once the original notions had been intuited, the rest was incontestable: there could be no relativism about it. All scientific and even philosophical knowledge worked in this manner. Yes, in line with the strictures of phenomenology it was certainly grounded on intuition (historically speaking). But no, it was not relative, because it followed on from these original intuitions by logical steps that uncovered a structure that was in a way "already there," just waiting to be discovered.

Derrida was convinced that this argument contained an *aporia*, an internal inconsistency which remained irresolvable. And in arguing this in his Introduction to Husserl's *Origin of Geometry*, and in later works, he laid the basis for his philosophical attitude. For Derrida's "philosophy" is not a philosophy as such, it is rather a questioning of philosophy: an "interrogation of its very possibility." He questions the entire basis of philosophy and its ability to operate on its own terms. The whole structure of philosophy is flawed by an *aporia*, and as such it cannot be

18

consistent. This was more than an obscure argument about the basis of geometry: it questioned
the possibility of philosophy itself. And as such,
the grounds of *all* knowledge.

According to Derrida, Husserl saw geometry
as a form of perfect knowledge, which existed in
a realm of timeless truth. It was incontestable
and remained true regardless of human apprehension or intuition. For Derrida, any possible
prehistoric intuition was irrelevant to the way
geometry had come to be regarded in history, as
the paradigm of all scientific and philosophical
truth. This was an ideal truth, beyond the realms
of argument. Derrida contested this. Even if the
basic concepts of this truth had been historically
(or prehistorically) intuited, the truth itself was
not grounded in lived experience. According to
Husserl, it had already existed "out there," waiting to be discovered. Hence *this* truth could not
possibly be grounded in lived experience. It was
not consciously intuited—the necessary grounding required by phenomenology for all knowledge. Here at the very heart of philosophy was
an *aporia*. By implication, our entire notion
of knowledge was inconsistent. Either our know-

ing was grounded in intuition, or it wasn't; it couldn't somehow be both. How do we *know* that geometry is "out there" waiting to be discovered? And surely we accept geometry as true because we apply logic to it, rather than intuit this? It may be logically consistent within its own terms, but how do we intuit it as knowledge? What basis in our consciousness—the ultimate grounding of our knowledge—do we have for accepting its truth?

Such questions may appear niggling, but their implications affect the whole of Western philosophy and the scientific knowledge that is based upon it. Heidegger had asked similar questions, and in doing so had revealed a hidden assumption that underlay the entire structure of our knowledge. And far from being grounded in individual intuition, this assumption was purely metaphysical. That is, it was somehow above and beyond our physical world. It wasn't based on experience of any sort. Heidegger showed that the whole notion of Western philosophy, and its attendant scientific knowledge, was based upon the idea that somehow, somewhere, truth itself could be validated in some absolute sense. There was a realm of truth that was not relative. The "somewhere out there" where geometry existed was part of a realm, "a presence," where absolute truth existed. It also guaranteed all truth. Here truth was validated by its own presence. It existed. (Otherwise it would have been an absence.) This presence was absolute, guaranteeing absolute truth. The identity of this existent presence can be none other than a form of being that knows all things and knows the truth of all things, including itself. This is the meaning of its truth. There is a coincidence of being and knowing in this presence which guarantees the truth of all things.

As Derrida would show, this guarantee of truth, this presence, reveals another *aporia*. The philosophical idea of a truth based purely on intuition falls victim to its own inner contradiction. Absolute truth can be guaranteed only by an absolute realm or presence. Any lesser finite truth must inevitably be relative. There is no way that a finite intellect, limited to its own intuition, can possibly know whether the truth of what it knows by intuition in any way matches the truth of what is. Such a coincidence, such an equality, could be guaranteed only by an absolute that it couldn't intuit.

It is not difficult to detect the ghostly presence of the divine behind the argument for "presence." For many centuries God had been the truth, guaranteeing such absolute truth. But without such a presence—call it divine or absolute—there is no truth, and we are left floundering in a quagmire of relativism. This applies to geometry as much as it does to philosophy. Indeed, Derrida would claim that such a state of affairs denies even the possibility of philosophy. Now it becomes clear why he doesn't see himself as a philosopher!

Philosophy had been down this road before. In the eighteenth century the Scottish philosopher David Hume accepted that all our knowledge was based upon experience. He then analyzed this seemingly uncontroversial empirical assertion and came to some surprising conclusions. Take such empiricism to its limits and our knowledge is reduced to ruins. We do not actually experience causality: instead of one thing causing another, all we actually perceive is one thing following another. Similarly we do not actually experience bodies, merely collections of sense data. We do not even experience our self. We have no direct experience of self, no impression that corresponds to identity, nor do we experience anything that tells us that this so-called self is identical from one moment to the next. Such trenchant reduction of truth to experience (a recognizable forerunner of phenomenological intuitionism) halted philosophy in its tracks. But it did not put an end to philosophy. It also did not put an end to human knowledge, especially science, which is based upon such notions as causality, identity, continuity, and so forth. All Hume had done was to demonstrate the *status* of our knowledge. When confronted with such rigid logical analysis, the illogic of our experience simply falls apart.

Philosophy may on occasion undermine the status of our knowledge completely. Theory can reduce its status to nothing. But this doesn't stop the *practice* of our attempts to gain it. This is certainly true in the fields of mathematics and "hard" sciences such as physics. We still attempt to gain knowledge in a scientific manner, even when anti-philosophers such as Heidegger and

Derrida succeed in exploding our entire notion of scientific truth. Perversely, we even continue to apply scientific method in fields that have yet to become established as science. Chaos theory demonstrates how the movement of a butterfly wing in the Brazilian rain forest can eventually result in a tornado in Kansas. The wildly differing effects of the many variables involved in meteorological forecasting are too incalculable for us to predict the weather far ahead with any certainty. The same applies to all economic predictions, as well as the workings of psychoanalysis. These are not yet sciences (and may never become so). But the fact is that we continue as best we can to apply scientific rigor in these fields.

Derrida's denial of geometric truth, of even the possibility of philosophy, is in its own abstract way subject to just the same strictures. In undermining truth he also succeeds in undermining the truth of what he is saying. As we shall see, Derrida would readily admit this—and would follow its implications through to daring and radical conclusions. But the fact is that such theory (whether or not it is sabotaged by its own contradictions) flies in the face of human practice. We practice economics and meteorology because the unfounded knowledge they produce helps us. We may accept that there is no such thing as absolute truth, no final guarantee for our knowledge—yet when all's said and done, we do not question that the three angles of a plane-surface triangle add up to 180 degrees. An electron within an atom is comparable in size to a needle in a football stadium, yet we have discovered exact calculations for precisely predicting its behavior. The entire computer industry relies upon such predictions. And we accept other, less mathematical scientific "truths"— such as Darwin's theory of evolution, the structure of DNA, and so forth. Indeed, even while accepting that there is no absolute truth, we paradoxically and fiercely oppose any attempt to undermine such "nonabsolute" truths by other than scientific disproof (i.e., experiment, experience). Truth may be relative in terms of absolute status, but treating it as relative is another matter. Derrida, for one, would presumably not deny the "truth" that millions of Jews died in the Holocaust. Western civilization may have developed using a self-contradictory notion of absolute truth, but without this self-contradictory notion it falls apart. Just how Derrida would come to terms with this, and the "impossibility" of philosophy, is vital to any assessment of his stature as a thinker.

In 1965 Derrida began teaching the history of philosophy at the École Normale Supérieure. By now he had become part of the group of emergent Parisian intellectuals associated with the avante-garde magazine *Tel Quel* (So What). Despite its flippant title, this was no lightweight gadfly journal. Its aim was to develop a new "intellectual terrorism" which would subvert all previous conceptions of writing, literary criticism, and philosophy. Among those who wrote for it at one time or another were all the leading new French thinkers: Barthes, Foucault, Kristeva, and Derrida. Inevitably, their initial loose-knit aims would soon diverge.

Derrida's aim was nothing less than to destroy all "writing" by demonstrating its inevitable falsehood. The writer writes with one hand, but what is he doing with the other? All writing, all texts, have their own hidden agenda, contain their own metaphysical assumptions. This is especially true of language itself. The writer often remains oblivious of this fact. The very language he uses inevitably distorts what he thinks and writes. In *Writing and Difference* (1967), Derrida attacked that epitome of French thought, the seventeenth-century rationalist Descartes, the first modern philosopher. By means of reason, Descartes had sought the ultimate intellectual certainty. In order to clear the ground, he had begun a process of systematic doubt. As a result he found that he could doubt the certainty of everything. His senses could deceive him, even his sense of reality sometimes couldn't distinguish between dreaming and waking. Likewise, a cunning malicious spirit could even be tricking him about the absolute certainty of mathematics. (And some three centuries later Derrida would claim to show how this could be the case.) But in the end Descartes found that there was one thing which he just could not doubt. This was the ultimate certainty *Cogito ergo sum* (I think therefore I am). No matter how he was deceived by the world, the one thing he couldn't doubt was that he was thinking.

Derrida disagreed. Basically he asserted that Descartes remained at the mercy of the language he used. It was impossible for him to reach "outside" the very language in which he thought—with all its hidden assumptions and its structure which constricted and distorted his thought. Its very dynamic and methodology was capable of leading his thought astray far more than any delusions of his senses. Such strictures were "inherent in the essence and very project of language, of all language in general." For instance, it was simply grammar that led Descartes to conclude: "*I* think therefore *I* am." His ultimate experience of certainty, as Hume would later show, contained no notion of identity or even causality ("*therefore* I am"). Ultimately Descartes was aware only of the coexistence of thought and being. Perhaps this thinking and existence were even identical. As Heidegger would later put it, our fundamental apprehension is "being-in-the-world"—this is the intuition of phenomenology, beyond reach of reason and science.

In another of his major works of this period, *Of Grammatology* (1967), Derrida elaborates the notions that have remained central to his

28

thinking. Vital to Derrida's attack on philosophy is undecidability. One of the deepest hidden assumptions of Western thought is the basic rule of logic, often referred to as the law of excluded middle. This concerns identity, and in its earliest form proposed by Aristotle it stated: "There is nothing between asserting and denying." In other words, a statement is either true or false. It cannot be neither, or both. Well before Derrida, exceptions had been noted to this rule. The proposition "This statement is a lie" defeats logic on its own ground. The proposition "He grinned fatly" can be seen as either empty of meaning (misapplication of categories) or poetically meaningful (to describe a chubby infant's smile). Indeed, all poetic statements, all images, all art even, contravenes the law of excluded middle. Take Shakespeare's "All the world's a stage / And all the men and women merely players." The world is certainly not a stage, made of wood and set up before an auditorium; and yet in another (imagistic) sense we play out the action of our lives just like actors on a stage. An image, like a picture, both is and is not what it portrays. Then there are statements that are metaphysical and thus unverifiable ("Beyond our universe lies eternity"); or ones that may be grammatically correct but remain empty of all meaning ("The curlicue cunningly crashes coronary crimping," "A pint of plain is your only man").

But Derrida went still further. He argued that previously philosophy had been mistaken in searching for essential truth that was somehow contained in the "essence of things." On the contrary, it should have concentrated on the language it uses. This does not have any essential equivalence with the objects or even the concepts that it names and describes. That is not how language achieves meaning. All we find in language is a system of differences, and meaning simply arises from these differences. Yet such differences are multifarious and subtle. There is no way in which the many shades of difference found in language can be reduced to a simple bedrock of logic that establishes identity.

Derrida claimed that Western thought, and especially philosophy, had been based upon the binary notion implicit in the law of excluded middle. Our defining concepts depended upon opposition. A statement was either true or false. A thing was either alive or dead. A location was either inside or outside, high or low, up or down, left or right. And so it went: positive/negative, good/evil, general/particular, mind/body, masculine/feminine—this was how we divided and classified our experience in order to give it meaning. One obvious objection to this method is that the meaning of one term depends upon the meaning of the other. In other words, the process is circular: it relates to itself rather than what it purports to describe. For Derrida this indicated the essential defect in such laws and their reasoning. They contained a hidden metaphysical assumption that they described some essential reality, and that this essential reality was characterized by a logical coherence. The reasoning found in logic was also found in reality. Such thinking not only assumed an essential reality—in the "presence" of an absolute truth—but also that this reality was logical. The entire notion of an absolute truth that contradicted the laws of logic was inconceivable.

Consciousness, our intuition of the world, is beyond logic. It intuits no "presence" of ab-

31

solute truth. We know ourselves and the world through consciousness and the "mirror of language." They are the grounding of our knowledge, what makes it possible. Yet this process, beyond reason and logic, is in fact *excluded* from the process by which we obtain knowledge—logic, reason, and so forth. The differences that give rise to meaning in language are transformed by logic into distinctions, identities, truths. For Derrida this contradiction inevitably undermines the "truth" of knowledge.

According to Derrida, our knowledge of the world, based upon identity, logic, and truth, stems from an *aporia*. It is the result of an inner contradiction. Once again, it is easy enough to point out Derrida's self-contradiction here. If the presence of a contradiction invalidates our logical knowledge, then surely the use of logic in Derrida's argument is equally damaging.

Despite Derrida's argument shooting itself in the foot in this fashion, the argument itself is not new. Even before Hume, the seventeenth-century Irish empiricist philosopher Berkeley managed to "disprove" mathematics—to his own satisfaction, by using mathematics. He pointed out a

32

number of inconsistencies which could only be rectified by introducing arbitrary rules into this system that apparently consisted solely of necessary truths. Thus mathematics was not logically certain. For instance:

12 x 0 = 0
13 x 0 = 0
Therefore: 12 x 0 = 13 x 0
Divide both sides by 0
Therefore: 12 = 13

According to Berkeley, this anomaly could be rectified only by introducing the arbitrary rule that you can multiply by 0 but not divide by it. More damagingly, Berkeley also pointed out the inherent *logical* flaw in Newton's calculus. Either the "infinitesimals" that Newton employed existed, or they didn't: his calculus switched in mid-calculation from one to the other. And despite his considerable use of the law of excluded middle in this argument, Berkeley also went on to "disprove" this law too (also with the use of logic). These exposures of flaws in the certainty of mathematics, and thus all "certain" knowledge, reached their apotheosis around the time of Derrida's birth. In 1931 the Austrian mathematician Gödel managed to prove, again by mathematical-logical methods, that mathematics could never be certain. Any rigidly logical system, such as mathematics, is bound to contain certain propositions that can neither be proved nor disproved by use of the basic axioms on which that system rests. This was in fact far more damaging to mathematics than anything Derrida was to produce, because it indicated the possibility that mathematics itself is capable of giving rise to mathematical contradictions. (It also broke the law of excluded middle. Such propositions were neither true nor false within the system.)

As we have seen, Derrida wished to go one step further, by invalidating the *entire process of logic*. And despite his protestations to the contrary, he did this by using logical argument. What Derrida adds that is essentially new to the 250-year-old arguments of Berkeley and Hume, or the "final" argument of Gödel, is debatable. And it is arguable that the distinction between intuition and rational thought reaches back over two thousand years to the earliest Greek era of philosophical thought. Derrida would of course argue that intuition and reason are simply not applicable, one to the other. Or at least that such application does not produce the certainty that is claimed for it.

Mathematics and science were able to survive Berkeley and Hume, and have continued regardless since Gödel. Derrida's strictures would seem to be equally effective. So what does this indicate? It was indeed a surprise, and a great blow to mathematical pride, to discover that mathematics was not quite as certain as it was assumed to be. For science it was another matter. Quite simply, *science was well aware of this all along.* Or at least has been increasingly so since the time of Galileo. Scientific theories are proposed, then modified (or scrapped altogether) when they conflict with reality (experimental findings). Scientific truth has not been absolutely certain, or seen as such by scientists, for some centuries now. Galileo was modified by Newton; Newton in turn was replaced by Einstein. Science is truth that works, not truth that is certain. And the same can be said, perhaps to a lesser degree, of all human knowledge. Derrida argues that we ignore the point here. For most of us the "presence" of some absolute truth lingers on in our attitude to knowledge. Such argument does not bear closer examination. As in science, so in the lesser certainties of history. Where such things as historical fact—the Holocaust, for example—are concerned, we behave *as if* the "presence" lingers on. We accept this event as true because of evidence, which of its very nature is open to interpretation, modification, or even contradiction. We accept the Holocaust as scientifically certain, not absolutely so.

But Derrida's purpose here is not entirely negative. Far from it. His main avowed aim is to *include* those very elements that logic and clarity sought to exclude from the rich flow of our conscious intuition.

In reducing our experience to such knowledge we exclude the full richness of what our experience is. Again, this insight is scarcely original. Knowledge is abstract—it *abs-tracts* from experience. The original Latin meaning of abstract is "to draw" (*traction* has the same root) "out of" or "away from" (as in absent). In other words, by implication, to reduce the whole.

36

Again, the process was initiated in human experience not in order to discover some absolute truth but in order to survive, to *make use* of experience, to gain power over the world around us. It was technical, scientific—before its much later pretensions to "absolute truth."

But Derrida's central argument here does concern how we use our knowledge, be it intuitional or so-called logical. How do we express ourselves and our knowledge? In language. But this too is not absolute, precise, or logical. Every word, every phrase, and even the way we place them in sentences, begets blurring ambiguities. Language eludes clarity and precision. Every word has its own meaning, or meanings. But it also brings with it any number of more or less hidden connotations. There are puns, echoing similarities, suggestive references, diverse interpretations, divergent roots, double meanings— and so on. Spoken language may allude to the double meanings in its intention. The comedian places camp emphasis on the innocent remark that is open to a far from innocent interpretation. Some statements may, under certain circumstances, even unwittingly convey their opposite. ("There will be no whitewash at the White House.")

Likewise with written language. The reader is free to add his own interpretation, attitude, intention. The words on the page—ambiguous in themselves—are merely a sounding board for the reader's interpretation. Derrida carries this analysis to its extreme. Difference without "positive terms" of identity means that language at this underlying level of meaning is almost completely fluid. If there is no identity, there are no concepts—such identifying notions are literally inconceivable. This level—amongst the fluidity of puns and jokes, of meanings blending into one another, and so forth—eludes clarity. But in doing so it also eludes to metaphysical "presence" of absolute truth that Western thought seeks to impose upon language. At this level—analogous in some ways to the unconscious mind—language retains its rich creative mix of undecidability amongst its differences.

Once again, the element of ambiguity in language has been clear to poets since literature began. This perhaps accounts for the first reception of Derrida's ideas in America, which he presented in a speech at Johns Hopkins University in 1966. Here Derrida's treatment of language was seen as an incisive and original tool for literary criticism. This showed how all kinds of new references and meanings could be discerned in a literary text, creating their own subtexts. It could reveal hidden intentions, covert metaphysical assumptions, and implicit ambiguities. On the other hand, Derrida's reception in the philosophical community was less enthusiastic. What was he trying to say?

Derrida's answer to this question eludes precision in much the same way as language, in Derrida's view, eludes precise meaning. But language *does* have a meaning. It originated as a means of communication. Even if that communication was only demonstrating inarticulate power—of the speaker over the hearer, as in primitive shouting—the intent was to communicate. And this communication of more or less precise meaning has remained its central activity. Literature, as art, continually plays with language and utilizes its playful, ambiguous element. But even this seldom descends into complete nonsense (non-sense). Dadaism, surrealism, and similar isms derive their power from dislocated meaning, anomalous evocations, and such. If they didn't, each "meaningless" text would have the same effect.

So of what use *is* Derrida's analysis? He exposes how the meaning of a text assumes various conventions and contains its own codes. He shows *how* a text achieves meaning, rather than *what* it means. He shows how the text is simplified. This method of limiting and manipulating the rich scope of language has always been the case, and is discernable amongst the earliest philosophers. Derrida illustrates this with an example from Plato's *Phaedrus*. In this, Plato relates the myth of the ancient Egyptian god Theuth, who explained to the king of Egypt the benefit of teaching his subjects how to write. This would enable his subjects to improve their memory and increase their wisdom. Theuth claimed: "My invention is a medicine [*pharmakon*] for fortifying both memory and wisdom." But the king objected that writing would produce the very opposite effect: "This invention will produce forgetfulness in the souls of those who have learned it because they will not need to exercise their memories, being able to rely upon what is written." Theuth had merely discovered a *pharmakon* for reminding, not for memory itself. Similarly with wisdom. The king pointed out that writing would merely produce the appearance of wisdom, not its reality. It would encourage the delusion of wisdom, not actual inner wisdom.

Derrida points out that Plato's myth contains a typical use of binary opposites, of either/or. *Either* writing is good for memory, *or* it isn't. Yet it could in fact be both. Derrida now focuses on the word *pharmakon*. In Greek this means "medicine," "cure," or "potion." (This is the origin of pharmacy.) But *pharmakon* can also mean "poison," "bewitchment," or "enchanting spell." The word *pharmakon* thus covers both sides of the argument. Writing can strengthen the power of memory, and it can also drug its powers. The meaning of *pharmakon* becomes unstable in this context, and this instability introduces *différence*. Identity, binary opposites, either/or—these are eliminated, and instead we have the ambiguity of difference. The logic of Plato's argument now begins to unravel, and instead we have undecidability.

Not surprisingly, American philosophers were somewhat less than impressed by Derrida's thinking here. Such treatment may have been all very well for literature, but what on earth did it have to do with the clarity of philosophical argument? It sought only to muddy the waters, blur the issues, take apart the concepts. Philosophy sought to eliminate such ambiguity. What was the point of trying to reintroduce it? Derrida countered such objections with two arguments. His attempt was to show the conventions by which philosophy operates, its assumptions of truth, its hidden codes. Second, he pointed out that all language was built upon this subtext of ambiguity. It eluded identity with any real object, and to ignore this was to ignore the fullness of what language *is*. The philosophers were not the only ones to remain underwhelmed by this argument. Scientists simply regarded it as trivial nonsense. A scientific law is valid until it is disproved—not by the introduction of verbal ambiguities. Lawyers and political thinkers dismissed

Derrida's arguments as a joke. Just as Derrida had indicated: each, in his context, retained his own conventions and assumptions. How much they were already aware of this, and how much this mattered, was another matter.

Derrida called his process of argument or philosophical approach (categorize it how you will) "deconstruction." This explains with some precision what he does. He takes apart what has implicitly already been put together in a text. The monumental authority of a text is disassembled. Instead of one meaning, it takes on many. After Derrida's first American lecture at Johns Hopkins, deconstructionism quickly began to catch on as an intellectual doctrine. Deconstruction, undecidability, *aporia*, *différence*, and the like quickly became the buzz words of the new campus cult. Johns Hopkins and Yale embraced deconstructionism with some enthusiasm; other institutions rejected it with equal passion. This split in American academia was soon echoed throughout the world. On the whole, French and Continental European philosophers were willing to listen. Britain and other anglophone countries were dismissive. This binary oversimplification reverberated through different disciplines. Derrida found his followers in philosophy and literary criticism; the sciences regarded it all as so much nonsense. There was no room for relativism in the domain of relativity.

In May 1968 Paris was overtaken by "Les Événements" (literally the incidents, or events). Students took to the streets in conflict with the police, and the Left Bank became the scene of vicious day and night riots. The students resisted the tear gas and water cannons of the riot police, erected barricades, flung cobblestones, and eventually took over the Sorbonne, effectively controlling the center of Paris south of the Seine. The trouble quickly spread to universities throughout France, and sympathetic spontaneous strikes broke out in several large factories. The country was brought to a virtual standstill. Many supported the students but feared the collapse of the state. The explosion of youthful violence arose as a result of years of authoritarian state rule, culminating in the sterility resulting from ten years of patriarchal government by the aging General Charles de Gaulle. In America,

Britain, Germany, and elsewhere, the social and cultural transformations of the sixties were under way. Mass demonstrations against nuclear weapons and the Vietnam War, the revolution in social mores accompanying the arrival of rock music and the hippie movement, as well as the advent of postwar affluence had brought little change in France. The educational system, especially, maintained a strong grip on young people. The school curriculum was rigid in the extreme, culminating in the dreaded *baccalauréat* exam which marked out success or failure for life. Indeed, the curriculum was so fixed that the minister of education could be certain, at any given hour on any given day, precisely which page of which textbook was being studied in every classroom throughout the land. By contrast, the situation in further education was a shambles—with the minimum of outmoded equipment, lecture halls so overcrowded that often half the students couldn't even get in; irrelevant and useless courses conducted by aged and inept professors; and impoverished living conditions.

The new post-Sartre wave of Parisian thinkers—such as Foucault, Barthes, Derrida, and others associated with *Tel Quel*—represented the intellectual protest against the sterility of French society. In such a context it is easier to understand some of the excesses of this movement. Derrida's insistence upon the "fluidity" of language becomes more comprehensible when seen against a background of the authoritarian edicts of the French educational system. His insistence upon the "difference" of language, instead of the identity of words with their subjects, subverts the prevailing linguistic orthodoxy. This was, and still is, the preserve of the Académie Française, which continues to deliver its pronouncements on French linguistic purity (such as the exclusion of "Americanisms" and other English words) and the *precise* meaning of French words. Such constraint produces an intimate sense of oppressiveness. It strikes at the very way one thinks, reaching into the mind itself. English-speakers, whose language is under no threat and every day penetrates further into the languages of the world, can have little or no experience of such problems. On the contrary, English has retained its far-flung homogeneity precisely through its ability to adapt, absorb, and withstand. (By contrast, consider the fate of Arabic. Classical Arabic script remains comprehensible from Morocco to the Philippines; yet spoken variants of Arabic can be all but incomprehensible from one country to the next.) By the middle of the twentieth century, American English had begun breathing new life into the moribund formality of the English English that was the lingua franca throughout the British Empire (over a third of the globe). And, arguably, that same English English had already contributed a range of articulacy and discipline to the fecund variety of American, Indian, Australian, and African variants, holding the whole together. Precisely this fact has prompted many of Derrida's American critics to see his strictures on language, and their philosophical implications, as irrelevant to the English-speaking world. We already know how language can take on a life of its own, how words can acquire new cadences or even entirely new meanings. One has only to consider such words as *gay*, *freak*, or *challenged* to see how English is in a constant state of flux. Derrida was in many ways fighting for a freedom that English-speakers take for granted. Yet this was of course not his central aim—which was to show that *all* language was fluid *through and through*.

At the outset of May 1968 Derrida played an active role, taking part in the marches and demonstrations. He even organized an assembly at the École Normale Supérieure, where open debates were held among students, sympathetic members of staff, and visiting trendy celebrity intellectuals who wished to jump on the bandwagon. Sartre himself was present at one of the assemblies in the Sorbonne, but he was soon howled down. His sympathies may have been with the students, but in truth he had now lost contact with this generation. The old had no real idea of the aspirations of the young. Even Derrida soon found the anarchy, the inarticulateness of demands and speech, the populism and the often determined philistinism, difficult to grasp. The force of youthful feelings that blossomed into such graffiti as "Beneath the street lies a beach," "Tomorrow shines on today," and "We are the writing on the wall" had no place for an intellectual agenda. (This had been Sartre's misunderstanding.) Derrida maintained sympathy, but he also maintained a low profile. What could he say amidst the uproar of the moment?

The world looked on in bemusement as the major cultural capital of the world was turned into an anarchist jamboree. Meanwhile de Gaulle panicked and secretly fled to Germany to consult with his military leaders (in command of the occupying French troops in the French zone of former West Germany). De Gaulle received the backing of the military, and the disorganized rebellion fell apart as the students set off for their holidays in the Greek islands. But the lesson had been learned. The old days were over. De Gaulle resigned within a year, and died a year after that. France entered the modern world— embarking on the road to populist democracy and youth culture. Workers were granted higher wages, and students were given a say in education. Derrida's lectures at the École Normale Supérieure became increasingly popular. The dashingly handsome natty dresser with the striking upswept hairstyle became a cult figure.

But this status was not achieved without a few ruffled feathers in the hothouse aviary of Parisian intellectual life. Derrida initially showed

sympathy for the views of his contemporary
Foucault, who also cut a dashing figure with his
trademark shaven head, designer spectacles, and
pale polo-neck sweaters. Foucault's cultural relativism was in accord with Derrida's linguistic
relativism. Both were seen as leaders of the
movement known as post-structuralism, which
regarded all knowledge as textual (i.e., a rela-
tivistic interpretation of text). History, psychology, philosophy, anthropology—all these dealt
not so much with concepts but with words. For
Foucault this led to epistemes (or paradigms) of
knowledge in which power was invested. These
structured the thinking of any given age, direct-
ing the way in which it thought, and thus deter-
mining what it thought about, the aims of its
thought, the lacunae of that thought, even ruling
out the possibility of thinking in certain ways.
For instance, the medieval era, which believed
that the world ultimately consisted of earth, air,
fire, and water, and mixtures thereof, simply
could not conceive of atomic elements. With the
advent of each new era—such as the transforma-
tion from the Renaissance to the Age of Reason—an entirely new episteme of thought was

established. Foucault saw Descartes as the epitome of the Age of Reason. After using reason to doubt everything, to unpick the very fabric of his existence (and by implication the certainties of the previous age and its episteme), Descartes had arrived at his basic certainty: "I think therefore I am." But Derrida took issue with Foucault's analysis. In using the language of reason to describe Descartes's method, Foucault had himself subscribed to the episteme of the Age of Reason. Descartes's doubt had in fact unwittingly undermined the very reason it sought to establish as paramount. Reason too could be doubted. Descartes's text was open to a far more drastic interpretation than the one placed on it by Foucault. It was a delusion to assume that thought can use a language that stands "outside" the very language it describes.

Foucault not surprisingly reacted with some passion to this critique, which threatened to undermine his entire intellectual project (and, it would seem, any other intellectual project). In Foucault's view, Derrida's nit-picking attack was just an intellectual game. This spat eventually led to a split in the entire post-structuralist approach. While Foucault retained the emphasis on the text, especially the historical document, he insisted that it was possible to analyze the power structure adhering to a particular text. The episteme that controlled and limited its writing implied a system of political power. Such a historical text was open to a particular interpretation. Derrida insisted that, like any text, it was open to a multitude of interpretations. The view of any historical document was liable to change from age to age. This may have freed the text from a single authoritative interpretation, but it left Derrida open to the charge that such a text could seemingly be given *any* interpretation.

Derrida's divergence of opinion from his Parisian contemporary Roland Barthes was less violent and apparently less fundamental. Barthes was the champion of semiology, whereby a text is studied for its "second order" meaning. Intellectual innocents who read a text in order to discover its author's intentions were dismissed as hopelessly naive. The real meaning of any text lay in an analysis of the symbols and interconnected signs whose structure underlay the surface. Barthes daringly extended such analysis far beyond the texts of philosophy and literature, into such diverse realms as fashion, the Eiffel Tower, and even wrestling (where all manner of interconnected signs were to be found grappling beneath the surface).

This method of analyzing texts led Barthes to announce the "death of the author." What he (or she) said didn't count. The author was merely a cultural construct: the product of an age, class, sex, socially determined expectations and appetites, and so forth. At its best, Barthes's analysis showed how surface language could overlay a hidden structure of assumptions, making these wholly artificial assumptions appear "natural," "universal," or even inevitable. This was the case, for instance, with the bourgeois novel and the unquestioned cultural values upon which it rested.

Derrida had mixed feelings about the so-called "death of the author." He naturally applauded Barthes for stripping bare hidden assumptions and revealing how the "universal truths" of bourgeois values were in fact no more than an arbitrary construct of prejudices and assumptions. This coincided with his own deconstructionist approach. Here was more evidence of the transcendental "presence" of Western metaphysics. It was always necessary to expose such "truth" as purely humanistic. On the other hand, Derrida deplored any assumption that such criticism itself could go beyond the humanistic and, so to speak, emerge "on the far side" of humanistic ideology, that one day it would be possible to make judgments entirely free from humanism and its inevitable bias. This was impossible. The very language in which such criticism was couched would inevitably contain traces of the humanistic assumptions on which it was based, on which it had grown throughout its history. This argument may appear somewhat circular, but its point was clear enough. We are bound within the circularity of our discourse. Our speech will always be subject to the language we use. We can never step outside its inevitably humanistic coloring. This may appear depressing with regard to any notion of truth beyond the socially agreed construct. Yet it does have distinctly heartening implications. The truth as we know it, in the only way we can know it, must remain humanistic. It must remain "of the human, for the human." Unfortunately, as recalcitrant deists and metaphysicians have been quick to point out, the same can be said of the metaphysical and religious assumptions that have for so long been a part of language. Derrida argues that we must get rid of this "presence," yet at the same time he argues that we can never get rid of the humanist "presence." It is difficult to see how he can have it both ways—except of course in the realm of "free interpretation" he advocates, which is presumably free to contradict itself.

By the late 1960s Derrida was becoming an increasingly celebrated presence himself. On both sides of the Atlantic his new deconstructionism was becoming equally fashionable—and equally controversial. Not only philosophers and scientists dismissed his ideas as obvious, needlessly complex, or incomprehensible nonsense. (One well-known English academic even went so far as to claim that his work was all three—a categorization which even Derrida himself might have had difficulty in deconstructing.) At the same time, Derrida's former students were becoming a pervasive influence far beyond the confines of Yale and Paris. But the forces of reaction had begun to close ranks. In most of the older universities, on both sides of the Atlantic, there was no room for deconstruction. The death of the author could take place elsewhere: the death of *these* authors had been greatly exaggerated.

In 1970 Derrida's mother died of cancer at the age of seventy. The following year Derrida returned to Algeria for the first time since the country's independence, delivering a series of lectures at the University of Algiers. During his stay he took the opportunity to visit the seaside villa where he had been born, his kindergarten, and many other sites of childhood memory. His "nostalgeria" was from now on to be rendered all the more poignant by the death of his mother. Cryptic references to these sites of his former life, and oblique indications of his feelings about them, now began appearing with increasing frequency in his work. But why this elusiveness when he had nothing to hide? Apparently to express such feelings directly would have been to diminish them. Their vitality would have been limited only by trying to contain them in words, which would have come between the actuality of his memories. Once again we have the *phar-makon*, which both cures and poisons, betrays and stimulates our memory. The *pharmakon*, or writing, is like a joker, the wild card in the pack. It can signify anything. Words are difference, not identity. We should be looking at how much words can signify, not attempting to see *what* they signify. Derrida wishes to keep his memories intact: the reason for his willful elusiveness with regard to autobiography becomes clearer.

In his ensuing works Derrida demonstrated with a vengeance his attitude toward clarity in language. In 1972 he once again produced three books. These were *Margins of Philosophy*, *Positions* (consisting of several interviews), and *Dissemination*. The latter was indicative of the direction Derrida's thought was now taking. *Dissemination* argues once again that there can never be a single fixed meaning to any text. The force of different meanings, puns, associative ambiguities, and similar features is irresistible. This causes a dissemination of meanings, of different interpretations. Derrida makes great play of the fact that the word *dissemination* contains echoes of "seme," the ancient Greek word for meaning (hence our word *semantics*). He also points out that it has echoes of "semen," thus it ejaculates meaning. The final essay in *Dissemination* was called "Dissemination." Derrida himself proudly proclaimed that this text was "undecipherable" and "unreadable"—thus forestalling the hapless critics. But this alas was the point. Here Derrida achieved an apotheosis of "textuality"—the play of differences in meaning, association, undecidability, and so on, ad incomprehensum. Two random examples. First a heading: "The Double Bottom of the Plupresent." Then a sentence: "Expropriation thus does not proceed merely by a ciphered suspension of voice, by a kind of spacing that punctuates it or rather draws its shafts from it, or at it; it is also an operation *within* voice."

No brief quotes can possibly do justice to the full extent to which Derrida here managed to elude all meaning in his text—all sense, all sanity even. Likewise any attempt to give an exegesis of the text is doomed to failure. Indeed, in the view of its author, to do so would only do a serious disservice to the text. The attempt to give it *a* meaning would merely eliminate any past meanings that it might have contained, as well as the possibility of any future interpretations. Any present meaning imposed upon the text can only be an illusion which attempts to reimpose the "presence" of some absolute meaning, some absolute truth—which is of course a fallacy. Or, to put it in the maestro's inimitable words: "Each time, writing appears as disappearance, recoil, erasure, retreat, curling up, consumption." All this is perhaps best illustrated by a description of what the text is and how it came into being.

Derrida's self-styled "essay" began life as a book review of *Numbers* by the contemporary French writer Philippe Sollers, another member of the *Tel Quel* group. *Numbers* baldly claims in its frontispiece to be a novel. It opens with a dedication in Russian, followed on the next page by an epigraph in Latin suggesting the book's limitless heights and depths of interpretation ("Seminaque innumero numero summaque profundo"). The text itself then starts straight in: ". . . the paper was burning, and there was some question of all things drawn and all paintings projected there of the regularly distorted manner, while a

phrase was saying: 'there is the external surface.'" A hundred pages later it closes with the words: "burnt and refusing to put the lid back on its squared space and depth—$(1 + 2 + 3 + 4)^2 = 100$ _____ [in Sollers's text this space is occupied by two large Chinese ideograms] _____."
In between, Sollers's "novel" is nothing if not novel. Yet this double negative can, and does, suggest almost anything. Here we find more Chinese ideograms, diagrams, and even puzzles, all contained in a series of largely inconsequential slabs of text, which are said to be related like the shards of a broken mirror. The text also contains quotes from such disparate figures as the seventeenth-century mathematician and religious zealot Pascal; Karl Marx; the medieval cardinal and prophetic scientific thinker Nicholas of Cusa; Friedrich Nietzsche; and Mao Tse-tung. Quotes are also included from Bourbaki, the pseudonym adopted by a varying group of French mathematicians who anonymously assume collective responsibility for the somewhat controversial axiomatic mathematical work produced under this name. Bourbaki's pure axiomatic approach stresses that in mathematics

one does not know what one is talking about, neither does one care whether what one says is true in any real sense. The resemblance to the text is presumably intentional, and aptly characterizes Derrida's method.

The same cannot be said of Wittgenstein, who is also quoted in *Numbers*. Wittgenstein's philosophic aim was if anything diametrically opposed to that of Derrida. Both admittedly claimed to have found the "final solution" to philosophy, thus putting an end to this subject once and for all. And both found the key to this lay in language. Yet here all resemblance ends. Derrida solved "the problem of philosophy" by the simple expedient of exploding language from the inside, detonating its meaning into myriad fragments of ambiguity, self-contradiction, and punny jokes. Any coherent philosophy—or coherent anything, for that matter—was thus rendered impossible. Wittgenstein, on the other hand, viewed philosophy as arising from the tangled knots of meaning arising when words were applied to inappropriate categories. (For example, it was simply impossible to ask "What is the purpose of life?" because such words as "purpose" and "life" could not be meaningfully applied to each other.) What we call philosophy arose only from mistakes in our use of language. When the knots were unraveled, the mistakes would simply disappear. Not only was there no answer to such philosophical questions, there was no question in the first place. What Wittgenstein and Derrida both had profoundly in common was their view of philosophy as a conjuring trick. But where Wittgenstein made the white rabbit in the hat disappear, Derrida produced an endless cornucopia of them.

Derrida's review of *Numbers* does little more than emulate the shattered mirror it claims to be reviewing. It is (to join in the spirit of things) a reflection with reflection, or reflections within a reflection. The original is quoted, mimicked, and even parodied (perhaps wittingly, but not wittily). Indeed, the original's obscurity seems to be taken as a challenge to be outperformed rather than overcome. It even claims that any review would be the same: "Some such other enumeration, altogether squarely written, would nevertheless remain undecipherable." Needless to say, some reviewers have managed to find a more direct way of expressing their opinion of Sollers's text and its attendant essay. "Bullshit" was the allegedly "undecipherable" opinion that sprang to the mind of more than one English-speaking reviewer. Even some of Derrida's closest admirers hoped that this work was an aberration. Where could he possibly go from here? What lay beyond the self-proclaimed "unreadable"?

The answer was not long in coming. Two years later, in 1974, Derrida published *Glas*. This work consisted of two continuous columns of print. Like *Dissemination*, these both begin in mid-sentence; but this time they go on for almost three hundred pages, with occasional indented passages like remarks, and occasional slabs of quotation. The left-hand column, with slightly larger print and closer-set lines, consists of a highly original reading of, and interweaving of quotes from, the nineteenth-century German philosopher Hegel. The other column is a commentary, also with extensive quotation, on the works of the French lyrical pederast writer and jailbird Jean Genet. Both are torturous in their own way. Yet the contrast between systematic German metaphysics and systematic French buggery could not be more extreme. No anti-German or homophobic intent is implied here. The works of both Hegel and Genet are on a par with Derrida in attacking the sensibilities and expectations of the mere reader. Hegel's page-long sentences of relentless metaphysical jargon qualify him as the de Sade of philosophy. Genet's relationship to de Sade is somewhat less philosophical, but the effect can be equally painful.

So what is *Glas* really about? As we should already be aware by now, the aim of all this is not for us to decide. In the words of Christopher Norris, one of Derrida's more sympathetic critics, "*Glas* is not a 'book,' at least in the traditional sense of that word: a volume whose unifying principle consists in its always referring us back to some privileged source of authorial intention." On the other hand, the typesetting and printing of this nonbook was evidently a matter of extremely precise intent to the privileged author. No take-it-or-leave-it limitless interpretation was permitted to the unfortunate printers. As many as four different type faces were employed in the text (one for each column, another for indentations, another for slabs of quoted text), to say nothing of frequent italics, passages in German, ancient Greek and Latin words, and so forth. And in its original printing this nonbook was assembled so that it had a volume of precisely one hundred cubic inches. Its pages were a square ten inches by ten inches, and these totaled one inch in thickness. I stress, *inches*. (What the French printers, who worked in centimeters, made of all this might have made even Genet's ears sing.)

But since this book is presented for public consumption, it is legitimate to question whether it means anything at all. Hegel's celebrated dialectical method began with a thesis, which then generated its own antithesis, and these two then merged to form a synthesis. For example: "Being" generates its antithesis "nothingness," and these then synthesize into "becoming." Hegel's entire all-embracing system is generated in this fashion. It is possible to read such dialectic at work in *Glas*. The left-hand Hegelian column becomes the thesis: an example of high philosophy at its highest, Hegel's ultimate intellectual justification for the authoritarian nineteenth-century Prussian state. And it is not difficult to read the antithesis of this in Genet's rhapsodies on "un jeune garçon blond" (a young blond boy) and "Divine aime Gabriel, surnommé l'Archange. Pour l'amener à l'amour, elle mette un peu de son urine dans ce qu'elle lui donne à boire ou à manger" (the Archangel Gabriel's urine being used as a love potion). The synthesis presumably takes place elsewhere, possibly in the mind of the reader. Or, as Derrida so tellingly puts it: "Its interpretation directly engages the whole Hegelian determination of right on one side, of politics on the other. Its place in the system's structure and development . . . is such that the displacements or disimplications of which it will be the object could not have a simply local character."

One could be forgiven for concluding that there has to be a limit to this kind of work. Once the "indecipherable . . . unreadable" has been produced in one form or another, its purpose is surely served. Derrida did not agree. Despite jetting around Europe to deliver speeches, holding down his academic post in Paris, and simultaneously fulfilling further academic duties at various universities in America, he continued to be stu-

pefyingly prolific. Even by this stage, his pro-
duction of "texts"—ranging from book-length
nonbooks to nonarticulate articles—ran into the
hundreds. What many consider to be his next
major work appeared in 1980. This was entitled
*The Post Card: From Socrates to Freud and Be-
yond.* The fact that Socrates had never sent a
postcard, to Freud or anyone else, stems from a
trivial deconstruction of this title, but one that is
valid nonetheless if one takes Derrida's method
at face value. Having got this funny joke out of
the way, we can now press on to the more serious joke of the text.

This begins with an essay on the "postal
principle." According to Derrida, this is of more
significance than Freud's pleasure principle, for
it covers the entire history of Western metaphysics "from Socrates to Freud and beyond." In
sending a postcard, or any message, we give
something but hold ourselves back from this giving. Great play is made of the relation between
the writer (*destinateur*) and the receiver (*desti-
nataire*), and the fact that these French words
contain links with "destiny" and "destination."
In writing earlier on this subject, Derrida had

reached the conclusion: "a letter can always not arrive at its destination . . . the structure of the letter [is] capable, always, of not arriving." The main part of the work is given over to an analysis of psychoanalysis. Freud's heroic attempt to raise psychoanalysis to the status of an empirical science is perversely dismissed as metaphysics—despite the fact that this was precisely what Freud was trying to avoid. But then, according to Derrida, *any* such attempt to establish truth is metaphysical, invoking the "presence" that has haunted all Western thinking. (The fact that Freud ultimately failed to establish psychoanalysis as a "hard" empirical science, like physics, is thus presumably laudable. In failing to free it from metaphysics, he didn't succeed in basing it on metaphysics.) Yet even in the midst of all this there are some difficult insights that appear worth the effort to unravel: "What is neither true nor false is reality. But as soon as speech is inaugurated, one is in the register of the unveiling of the truth as of its contract of properness: presence, speech, testimony." Speech, which incorporates truth and falsehood, describes a reality that does not incorporate such entities.

Philosophy's concern with that reality (or the grounds for our relationship with it) will always place it at one level deeper than science. In the last analysis, scientific knowledge merely seeks to describe our encounter with that reality rather than the reality itself (or the grounds for our contact with it). It records experimental evidence of our encounters. And here lies the difficulty with Derrida's analysis. The point about speech is that it involves our *encounter* with this value-less reality. A bottle of arsenic is in itself neither true nor false. The label "poison" on the bottle, either true or false, describes the reality of a possible encounter rather than the thing itself. This is a scientific truth, not an absolute truth. It is verifiable by experience, not by reference to any absolute "presence."

In 1981 Derrida's travels took him to Prague, which was then behind the Iron Curtain. Derrida had been instrumental in establishing the Jan Huss Association (named after the fifteenth-century Czech martyr who defied the power of the church). The aim of this association was to aid the repressed intellectuals of Czechoslovakia who were being persecuted by the Communist regime. At considerable risk to himself and his listeners, Derrida held a week-long seminar. This included a paper entitled "Before the Law," echoing the title of a short story by Kafka, who had lived most of his life in Prague. The meaning of this characteristically obtuse talk was nonetheless plain even to the secret police, who regarded the second syllable of Derrida's deconstructionism as superfluous. Derrida was searched, and a brown packet of marijuana was "discovered" in his possession. He was immediately locked up.

France takes its intellectuals very seriously, even when others find themselves unable to do so. What might have appeared to the Czech authorities as a minor incident involving a provocative French poseur was viewed very differently by the Parisian press. France's national heritage was at stake, and President François Mitterand himself was soon making his feelings plain to the Czech authorities in flagrantly undeconstructed language. (Twenty years earlier, when French authorities had sought to arrest Sartre for illegal political activity, de Gaulle himself had intervened, informing them, "You don't

arrest Voltaire." Sartre thus involuntarily em-
bodied his existentialism, which decreed: "Man
is condemned to be free.") Derrida was speedily
released by the Czech authorities and arrived
back in Paris to a hero's welcome. During the
previous year Sartre had died, as had Barthes.
Three years later Foucault would be dead, leav-
ing Derrida to assume the mantle—which had
passed from Descartes, through to Voltaire, and
on to Sartre—of France's greatest living intellectual.

Derrida had always seen deconstruction as a
tool for use against political authoritarianism
and injustice. Yet the "politics of deconstruction" would appear to resist any explicit manifesto or clear *constructive* action. According to
Derrida: "Deconstruction should seek a new in-
vestigation of responsibility, questioning the
codes inherited from ethics and politics." This
could of course lead to any political stance. Yet
despite such intellectual fence-sitting, Derrida
himself would play an active role during the
mid-eighties in the campaign to free Nelson
Mandela and end apartheid in South Africa.

More controversially, and more dangerously,

he also led a campaign against racism in France, a perennial feature of the local political scene which focused heavily on the large North African immigrant population. In the teeth of fierce opposition he campaigned for immigrant enfranchisement. "The combat against xenophobia and racism also goes via this right to vote. So long as it is not gained, injustice will reign, democracy will be limited to that extent, and the riposte to racism will remain abstract and impotent." The inheritor of Voltaire's mantle appeared to have inherited his predecessor's clarity of mind when it came to political argument.

Things were a little different when it came to the politics of feminism. If the binary opposites of Western logical thought—true/false, mind/body, positive/negative—were to be replaced by undecidability, what became of the male/female polarity? Women may have wished to be treated as equals (undecidability), but they also insisted upon their separate identity (polarity). The way out appeared to be to stress difference in place of identity. Like the logical polarity it reinforced, patriarchy should be deconstructed. But this shouldn't be applied to feminism itself. Feminists who sought equality with men were simply repeating the old mistakes. Such feminism "is the operation through which a woman desires to be like a man, like a dogmatic philosopher, demanding truth, science, objectivity. That is to say, with all masculine illusions." Derrida also opposes what he calls "reactive feminism," which is merely "adaptive and self-limiting." On the other hand, "active" feminism asserts difference, making it positive. Many feminists have seen all this as mere rhetoric, but Derrida and deconstructionism have nonetheless retained a strong American advocate in the person of Barbara Johnson (who managed the Herculean task of faithfully translating *Dissemination* into unreadable English).

In 1992 Derrida found himself at the center of a controversy in England. When Cambridge University offered him an honorary degree, his candidature was opposed by some members of the faculty—the first time such a thing had happened in living memory. His opponents didn't mince their words. French philosophy was run by "a system of mandarins and gurus and fashions [and] did not have the same standards of rigor and clarity" as its British counterpart. Indeed: "The French excel in fabricated terms of shifty meaning which make it impossible to detect at what point philosophical speculation turns to gibberish." Despite such Francophobic outbursts, Derrida was eventually awarded his honorary degree.

Derrida has continued with his deconstructionist program. As prolific as ever, he persists in engaging the great thinkers and writers of the past in his deconstructionist dialogue. Socrates, Plato, Descartes, Kant, Rousseau, Hegel, Nietzsche, Marx, and Mallarmé, to name but a few, have all taken part (or more accurately, been taken apart) in this one-sided process. Their work is deconstructed, translating their findings into deconstructionist code. A few brief examples will suffice, the reader being left to make up his own mind concerning the point of the exercise.

Freudian psychology: Derrida insists that the conscious mind is never free from "traces" of experience in the unconscious mind. The perceiving self, which imagines itself in the present, is in fact always being "written" by unconscious "traces" from the past, which in its turn is also being "written" by unconscious traces from *its* past, and so on and so on. This means that there is no such thing as a pure perception.

Never one to shirk difficulties, in 1991 Derrida decided to take on board Marx, at the very time when the collapse of Marxism appeared to have been final. In *Specters of Marx* he engages in what he calls "hauntology." This is the study of the ghosts, specters, and spirits that haunt the space between the binary opposites of being and non-being, the living and the dead. Great play is made of the fact that his invented word *hauntology* (*hantologie*) sounds the same in French, which has a silent "h" here, as ontology (*ontologie*). The latter is the sphere of philosophy devoted to thinking about "being," or ultimate existence. The opening sentence of Marx's *Communist Manifesto* reads: "A specter is haunting Europe, the specter of communism." For Derrida, Marxism is not alive (as was once believed) or dead (as is now believed). Instead of this polarity it is undecidable, a specter. Derrida finally decides that deconstruction is really a more radical form of Marxism. With this conclusion he succeeds in the all but impossible task of uniting almost the entire range of contemporary philosophers and political thinkers. Unfortunately he succeeds in uniting them against him. I say "almost": by this I mean all, except those who subscribe to the Parisian intellectual scene, where Derrida's conclusion is of course hotly contested both for and against (inspiring just the sort of polarity that Derrida himself adjudges to be invalid).

It was perhaps inevitable that Derrida would at one point focus on James Joyce, whose mastery of verbal sleight of hand is if anything the very opposite of Derrida's. Joyce's use of language is both readable and entertaining, adds richness of meaning to what it describes (without obliterating either its meaning or the object of its description), and carries no (anti-)philosophical agenda. "Is there a limit to the interpretations of Joyce?" asks Derrida. No, he decides. Then he appears to contradict this by explaining that Joyce has encompassed the possibility of all possible interpretations before us. Curiously, Derrida decided to tackle Joyce's *Ulysses* rather than *Finnegans Wake*, which might more easily have approached some agenda of infinite interpretation without ultimate meaning. As it is, even this aberration of genius has its impressionist drift of meaning beneath the blizzard of neologisms, puns, and solipsist solecisms:

"Three quarks for Muster Mark!
Sure he hasn't got much of a bark
And sure any he has it's all beside the mark."

Long before Derrida deconstructed Joyce, the American nuclear scientist Murray Gell-Mann was reading *Finnegans Wake* for pleasure. When Gell-Mann discovered a new species of subatomic particles he playfully decided to name them "quarks," selecting the word from the preceding quote. For Joyce the literary neologist, the word *quark* is open to a variety of punning and amusing interpretations. For Derrida it could doubtless be deconstructed to the point of meaninglessness. For Gell-Man, and now the entire scientific world, it is the precise name for a species of subatomic particles having a spin 1/2 and electric charge + 2/3 or – 1/3 units, which combine to form the hadrons but have not been detected in a free state. In the above parable of interpretations, one is a literary use of language, another is a scientific use. What, if anything, the other is remains entirely up to you (as, of course, Derrida would agree).

Derrida: Mixed Quotes and Mixed Reviews

When I speak, I am conscious of being present for what I think, but also of keeping as close as possible to my thought a signifying substance, a sound carried by my breath.

—Jacques Derrida

All attempts to define deconstruction are bound to be false. . . . One of the principal things in deconstruction is the delimiting of ontology and above all of the third person present indicative: propositions of the form "S is P."

—Jacques Derrida

As soon as "present speech" "bears witness" to the "truth of this revelation" beyond the true or the false, beyond what is truthful or lying in a given statement or symptom in their relation to a given content, the values of adequation or unveiling no longer even have to await their verification or achievement from the exterior of some object.

—Jacques Derrida

Derrida's deconstruction attempts to show that "everyday language is not neutral; it bears within it the presuppositions and cultural assumptions of a whole tradition. . . . Maybe this anti-populist yet anti-Platonic element . . . is Derrida's most important contribution."

—John Lechte

Derrida is alluding . . . to that long tradition in philosophy, from Plato to Heidegger, which has sought to establish grounds or foundations for reason itself. . . . Such grounds may turn out to be unavailable.

—Christopher Norris

It may be in the questioning of reason itself—a questioning nonetheless patient and meticulously argued—that philosophy can best live up to its present responsibilities.

—Christopher Norris

Derrida was considered by some "the most important philosopher of the late twentieth century. Unfortunately, nobody was sure whether the intellectual movement he spawned—Deconstruction—advanced philosophy or murdered it."

—Jim Powell

America is an immigrant nation, and as such has "a multiplicity of perspectives on life, language, and behavior that snobbish homogeneous France, suppressing its resident Algerians, lacks. Derrida, an Algerian Jew, had his own private agenda that is not applicable to America."

—Camille Paglia

Barthes is echoing Derrida's critique of "the theological simultancity of the book," the metaphysical presupposition that the essence of a text is a simultaneous network of reciprocal relationships, and thus that the dimensions of temporality and volume are purely contingent.

—Michael Moriarty

Deconstruction is a theory which appears to lend itself most readily to babbling obfuscation.

—Peter Lennon

Chronology of Significant Philosophical Dates

6th C B.C.	The beginning of Western philosophy with Thales of Miletus.
End of 6th C B.C.	Death of Pythagoras.
399 B.C.	Socrates sentenced to death in Athens.
c 387 B.C.	Plato founds the Academy in Athens, the first university.
335 B.C.	Aristotle founds the Lyceum in Athens, a rival school to the Academy.

324 A.D.	Emperor Constantine moves capital of Roman Empire to Byzantium.
400 A.D.	St. Augustine writes his *Confessions*. Philosophy absorbed into Christian theology.
410 A.D.	Sack of Rome by Visigoths heralds opening of Dark Ages.
529 A.D.	Closure of Academy in Athens by Emperor Justinian marks end of Hellenic thought.
Mid-13th C	Thomas Aquinas writes his commentaries on Aristotle. Era of Scholasticism.
1453	Fall of Byzantium to Turks, end of Byzantine Empire.
1492	Columbus reaches America. Renaissance in Florence and revival of interest in Greek learning.
1543	Copernicus publishes *On the Revolution of the Celestial Orbs*, proving mathematically that the earth revolves around the sun.
1633	Galileo forced by church to recant heliocentric theory of the universe.

1641	Descartes publishes his *Meditations*, the start of modern philosophy.
1677	Death of Spinoza allows publication of his *Ethics*.
1687	Newton publishes *Principia*, introducing concept of gravity.
1689	Locke publishes *Essay Concerning Human Understanding*. Start of empiricism.
1710	Berkeley publishes *Principles of Human Knowledge*, advancing empiricism to new extremes.
1716	Death of Leibniz.
1739–1740	Hume publishes *Treatise of Human Nature*, taking empiricism to its logical limits.
1781	Kant, awakened from his "dogmatic slumbers" by Hume, publishes *Critique of Pure Reason*. Great era of German metaphysics begins.
1807	Hegel publishes *The Phenomenology of Mind*, high point of German metaphysics.

1818	Schopenhauer publishes *The World as Will and Representation*, introducing Indian philosophy into German metaphysics.
1889	Nietzsche, having declared "God is dead," succumbs to madness in Turin.
1921	Wittgenstein publishes *Tractatus Logico-Philosophicus*, claiming the "final solution" to the problems of philosophy.
1920s	Vienna Circle propounds Logical Positivism.
1927	Heidegger publishes *Being and Time*, heralding split between analytical and Continental philosophy.
1943	Sartre publishes *Being and Nothingness*, advancing Heidegger's thought and instigating existentialism.
1953	Posthumous publication of Wittgenstein's *Philosophical Investigations*. High era of linguistic analysis.

Chronology of Derrida's Life and Times

1930	Born in suburb of Algiers.
1940	Algeria becomes part of Nazi empire.
1942	Camus publishes *The Outsider* and *The Myth of Sisyphus*. After introduction of racial laws and Jewish quotas in schools, Derrida is expelled. Mostly plays truant from unofficial Jewish *lycée*.
1943	Sartre publishes *Being and Nothingness*, introducing Heidegger's thought and existentialism to France.

1950	Derrida goes to Paris to prepare for entry to École Normale Supérieure.
1951	Break between Sartre and Camus over communism.
1952	Derrida finally passes exam for École Normale Supérieure.
1956	Awarded one-year scholarship to Harvard.
1957	Marries Marguerite Aucoutourier.
1957–1959	Military service in Algeria: serves as teacher in school for children of military.
1960	Suffers from bout of severe depression.
1960–1964	Teaches at the Sorbonne.
1962	End of Algerian War results in independence for Algeria. Beginning of Derrida's "nostalgeria." Writes first major work: long Introduction to his translation of Husserl's *Origin of Geometry*.
1963	First son, Pierre, born.

1965	Secures post teaching history of philosophy at École Normale Supérieure.
1967	Publication of three seminal works expressing his ideas: *Speech and Phenomena*, *Writing and Différence*, and *Of Grammatology*.
1968	"Les Événements" in Paris: in May students revolt and take over the Left Bank; President de Gaulle flees in secret to Germany.
1972	Takes part-time teaching post at Johns Hopkins University. From now on he divides his teaching between Paris and the United States.
1974	Publication of *Glas*.
1980	Publication of *The Post Card: From Socrates to Freud and Beyond*.
1981	Arrested by Communist authorities in Prague on trumped-up charge of carrying marijuana.
1984	Death of Foucault.

1987   Appointed visiting professor at University of California, Irvine.

1992   Controversy at Cambridge University, England, prior to his award of honorary doctorate.

Recommended Reading

Geoffrey Bennington, trans., *Jacques Derrida* (University of Chicago Press, 1999). This includes Derrida's autobiographical *Circumfession* in parallel with Bennington's comparatively lucid exegesis of the maestro's thinking processes.

Roland A. Champagne, *Jacques Derrida* (Twayne, 1995). A useful short overview of Derrida's thought, leading the author to "concluding the inconclusive."

Jacques Derrida, *Of Grammatology*, trans. G. C. Spivak (Johns Hopkins University Press, 1998). The masterful translation of Derrida's seminal early work. Difficult reading, with much jargon, but it gives a good picture of the "real stuff."

Jacques Derrida, *The Post Card: From Socrates to*

Freud and Beyond, trans. Alan Bass (University of Chicago Press, 1987). Derrida's major later work, both more approachable and more "enigmatic" than some of the more extended works.

Camille Paglia, *Sex, Art and American Culture: Essays* (Vintage Books, 1992). See the index for a wide range of references to Derrida and post-structuralism. Extreme, and extremely perceptive, criticism of the new wave of French thought from an American standpoint.

Julian Wolfreys, ed., *The Derrida Reader* (University of Nebraska Press, 1998). "Writing performances" from a wide range of Derrida's voluminous books, articles, interviews, commentaries, etc.

Index

Aristotle, 29
Aucoutourier, Marguerite, 15–16
Augustine, Saint, 10–11

Barthes, Roland, 26, 45, 52–53, 71, 81
Berkeley, George, 32–34, 35

Camus, Albert, 9, 13; *The Outsider,* 9; *The Plague,*
    11

Deconstructionism, 43–44, 53–55, 71, 73, 74, 81
Descartes, René, 27–28, 51, 71, 74

École Normale Supérieure, 13, 15, 26, 48, 49
Empiricism, 22–23, 32
Événéments, Les (1968), 44

Foucault, Paul-Michel, 26, 45, 50–53, 71

Genet, Jean, 63–64, 65, 66
Gödel, Kurt, 34–35

Hegel, G. W. F., 63–64, 65–66, 74
Heidegger, Martin, 6, 14, 20, 23, 28, 80
Hume, David, 22, 23, 28, 32, 34, 35
Husserl, Edmund, 14; *Origin of Geometry*, 16–20

Joyce, James, 76–77; *Ulysses*, 76; *Finnegans Wake*, 76–77

Kristeva, Julia, 26

Marx, Karl, 60, 74, 75; *Communist Manifesto*, 75

Newton, Isaac, 33, 35
Nietzsche, Friedrich, 6, 60, 74

Plato, *Phaedrus*, 40–42, 74, 80

Sartre, Jean-Paul, 14, 48, 70, 71
Sollers, Philippe, *Numbers*, 59–61, 62–63

Tel Quel magazine, 26, 46, 59

Wittgenstein, Ludwig, 61–62
Works: *Circumfession*, 10; *Dissemination*, 57–61, 62–63, 73; *Glas*, 63–65; *Margins of Philosophy*, 57; *Of Grammatology*, 28; *Positions*, 57; *The Postcard: From Socrates to Freud and Beyond*, 67–69; *Specters of Marx*, 75; *Writing and Difference*, 27

A NOTE ON THE AUTHOR

Paul Strathern has lectured in philosophy and mathematics and now lives and writes in London. A Somerset Maugham prize winner, he is also the author of books on history and travel as well as five novels. His articles have appeared in a great many publications, including the *Observer* (London) and the *Irish Times*. His own degree in philosophy was earned at Trinity College, Dublin.

NOW PUBLISHED IN THIS SERIES:

Thomas Aquinas in 90 Minutes
Aristotle in 90 Minutes
St. Augustine in 90 Minutes
Berkeley in 90 Minutes
Confucius in 90 Minutes
Derrida in 90 Minutes
Descartes in 90 Minutes
Foucault in 90 Minutes
Hegel in 90 Minutes
Hume in 90 Minutes
Kant in 90 Minutes

Kierkegaard in 90 Minutes
Leibniz in 90 Minutes
Locke in 90 Minutes
Machiavelli in 90 Minutes
Nietzsche in 90 Minutes
Plato in 90 Minutes
Sartre in 90 Minutes
Schopenhauer in 90 Minutes
Socrates in 90 Minutes
Spinoza in 90 Minutes
Wittgenstein in 90 Minutes

IN PREPARATION:

Bacon, Dewey, Heidegger,
Marx, J. S. Mill, Bertrand Russell